T0147733

THE
PRETENDING
WOMAN

Elizabeth A. Habbitt

authorHOUSE®

AuthorHouse™
1663 Liberty Drive
Bloomington, IN 47403
www.authorhouse.com
Phone: 833-262-8899

© *2020 Elizabeth A. Habbitt. All rights reserved.*

No part of this book may be reproduced, stored in a retrieval system, or transmitted by any means without the written permission of the author.

Published by AuthorHouse 03/27/2021

ISBN: 978-1-7283-5012-7 (sc)
ISBN: 978-1-7283-5011-0 (e)

Print information available on the last page.

Any people depicted in stock imagery provided by Getty Images are models, and such images are being used for illustrative purposes only. Certain stock imagery © Getty Images.

This book is printed on acid-free paper.

Because of the dynamic nature of the Internet, any web addresses or links contained in this book may have changed since publication and may no longer be valid. The views expressed in this work are solely those of the author and do not necessarily reflect the views of the publisher, and the publisher hereby disclaims any responsibility for them.

Don't think you are all alone in your problems. You don't know how many sleepless nights those around you may be having, but they may find it easier to pretend that everything is okay.

CONTENTS

Are you walking around depressed, thinking that the world is such a terrible place or that you have been dealt a really bad hand in life? Well, it's okay to have all of your private thoughts, but are they consuming you morning, noon, and night? Are you sleep-deprived, or are you looking for someone to listen to your complaining? Are you looking for peace through money, a mate, a bigger house, excessive shopping, a bigger car, a prestigious job, or all the things that the world system says will make you happy.

Well, if you feel you have been dealt a bad hand, why not go back and see if you can see when you started feeling this way? Have you thought about what may be the real underlying problem? You may be pretending that your life is so great, but in reality, you are super-frustrated by the thoughts you are carrying around as well as your true circumstances.

There are those who may feel that going to church every Sunday, and to midweek Bible study, prayer meetings, and reading the Bible means they will have perfect lives. There is no such thing as a perfect life. The sad part about it is that most people pretend that their lives are so different than they actually are to keep from being ridiculed by those around them. Sometimes people mean well, but many have their own struggles. But that does not stop them from giving you all kinds of unsolicited advice, suggestions that they won't even follow themselves.

INTRODUCTION

If you look around and see any woman, she's probably pretending about something. Someone may ask, "Why concern yourself? What's the big deal?" Actually, it could become a big deal because the things that you, or anyone else, pretend about could very well be things you need to deal with before they spiral out of control.

It doesn't matter what a woman's economic status is—rich, poor, middle class, between classes, whatever. She may be married, divorced, separated, estranged, or another category she puts herself in. She may be pretending about some area of her life. When you see someone, or a couple, who you perceive as perfect, take another look. Looks, especially first looks, can be deceiving.

This is not to say men are not big pretenders; some are. And about some of the same things. But in this book, we concentrate on women.

Women pretend mostly to impress their biggest critics, other women. Women criticize other women constantly. In reality, however, they may be in situations worse than the ones they criticize another woman for. When a woman criticizes another, she may actually be the person she is talking about. So don't go into a depression over someone who, in reality, may be living an artificial life.

What do I mean by artificial? The first things one may think about are all the fake eyelashes, nails, wig, weaves, dental implants, enlarged lips, enlarged butts, breast implants, and so on. This is not the artificial I mean. Those are just items that some women use to enhance their appearances. I'm speaking of those who spend their everyday lives pretending to be something they are not. All are artificial.

Look at all the couples you thought were so perfect but ended up in divorce court. That's not to say just because a couple doesn't get a divorce means they have a good marriage. But in many cases, the divorce was just the culmination of the effects of another problem. Do you know how many people are miserable but have decided to stay in a relationship? This is, of course, their choice for whatever reason. It's great to be in a healthy relationship, but not just because your finances won't allow you to do otherwise, or you are trying to keep up a fake front.

The purpose here is to inform you that you are not alone in whatever you are battling. There are others who are fighting the same battle. Keep in mind that nothing here is scientific or medical. I am just providing information gained through observation.

Now, let's take a look at some of the things that women pretend about.

1

Pretending Not to Eat This or That

How many times have you seen women who are always on an eating regiment? They can't eat this, or they can't eat that. It just flips and flops from one week to the other. One week they are not eating carbs, and the next week they are not eating this kind of meat or that kind of meat. The week after that, they are eating only salads and no dressing. And here's a really good one. They are sure if they just smell food, it makes them gain weight. They don't eat cookies or cake, pies or doughnuts, and certainly not candy.

This is not referring to someone who has a medical condition and restrictions recommended by a medical professional. It is about someone who eats all the above, but when she goes out in public, she gets a tiny salad. Look in the mirror, and you will know you didn't gain those extra pounds from eating those salads.

Why pretend? Just do you. It's not anybody's business what you eat or don't eat. Perhaps you could cut down on your portions or make healthier choices, but you don't always have to get that salad when you are out with friends or family. The best choice should be that you eat what you want in moderation, or follow whatever a health-care professional suggests to you. Those around you are not your doctor.

2

Pretending to Have More Money Than They Actually Do

This chapter does not refer to the truly wealthy. We know there are people who have plenty of money, but they may not have as much as they pretend to have. I'm speaking of the working-class person who has to work, invest in retirement programs, save to get a home, or perhaps was left a home by a parent or other relative or got the house in a divorce. In many cases, these still carry mortgages..

Many people become ensnared by someone they thought had more than they actually have. It's easy to be deceived by outward appearances. Many women have thought they were getting partners who were well-off financially to find later they had been dating pretenders, individuals who pretended to own things they did not. These women were baited by the fish.

Always look at one's actions, not his or her words.

3

Pretending to Have the Perfect Mate

How many women do you know who try to pretend they have the perfect mate or significant other? There is no such animal. Why pretend that your man doesn't do this or that? Don't tell people, "I wouldn't take this or that," because in reality, you may have taken something worse. But you've made it your so-called secret. It's really not a secret because you probably told someone. Or even worse, if you caught your man in the wrong, he probably told one of his buddies, who told one of his buddies. Men talk just like women, sometimes even more.

So always remember your secret is probably not a secret. The only way to guarantee something is a secret if you are the only who knows, and you don't tell anyone. I'm sure someone else knows your so-called secret.

It's probably not a good idea to make your mate out to be the perfect guy. Just go about your business being you. There's one thing for sure: Actions speak louder than words. You don't have to tell anyone that good meat makes its own juices. Others will be able to see it.

You don't have to entertain the perfect mate twenty-four hours a day. You also don't have to keep watch over him.

If you are experiencing these issues, you know it's a struggle. And it is likely those around you also know it, even if they never say anything to you about it.

You don't have to try and convince others that you are with the perfect mate. Just concentrate on being you and living your life. As with everything, time will tell. In many cases, sooner than later.

4

Pretending to Be the Family Favorite

Here's a really good one. How many women do you know pretend to be the family favorite. This could be an old line that people use quite frequently to make a family member feel special. Getting caught up on someone saying you are the favorite family member could just be a good way to make you feel special. Teachers may use this line to make their students feel special. They might say things like, "This is my favorite class," which will make those students feel good, empowered, or have positive attitudes toward their work, peers, and teachers. Even preachers sometimes make references to things like, "This early morning crowd really understands the sermon that I'm preaching today." Statements like these will make even a group of adults stick out their chests, even though the preachers will likely tell the next service the same thing.

5

Pretending to Be the Most Reliable Family Member

Have you ever given much thought to the question, "What are you the most reliable at doing?" If you look around, everyone is reliable at something. Maybe you are reliable at going to get the groceries for someone, while another person is reliable at making sure the plumbing is working and the grass is cut. Another person is reliable at making sure all the washing is done or the floors are mopped and vacuumed. Another is reliable at making sure someone gets to doctor appointments on time. Some people are just reliable at checking on a person to actually see how he or she feels, wanting nothing in return.

Therefore, I think we should be careful about saying we are the most reliable because you may be reliable, but no one can do everything. All parts of a body work together. It's known that many women are multitaskers, but all parts of the whole are important.

I once heard someone say that they knew a person who felt all of the relatives relied on this individual in times of need. Well, that may or may not be true. Some people have a need to believe that everybody needs them, when, in reality, they could be the people everyone wishes wouldn't show up to help.

6

Pretending Not To Be In An Abusive Relationship

Do you know anyone in an abusive relationship? You may know more people than you think. When we look at all the movements addressing women's issues, we rarely have a great number of women who will admit that they are being abused. The sad thing is that women will stay in an abusive relationship for all kinds of reasons. A woman may not leave because she feels her abuser is a good person, and in time, he will get better. The abuser may get better in time, or he may not. That's a gamble women who stay will have to take. Sure, they can stay with an abuser forever. And when they see in the mirror at how broken down they are, they may ask themselves, "Was it really worth it?"

Though people may not know exactly what's going on in your home, they probably know something is wrong. She may even have a nice car and clothes but living in pure hell at home.

It's hard to hide being abused. In reality, you are not saving face because an abuser is abusive everywhere in one form or another. An example is if a woman is always by herself but has a significant other. Well, where is he? Or a man is with a woman everywhere she goes. Typically, a man who is truly interested in his significant other does not want her always running around alone. But the abuser goes to the extreme. For example, she is too afraid to speak to anyone. Or she's accused of liking or flirting with every man that she comes in contact with.

This is not to say only men act like this. There are women who think that every woman wants their men because they are so insecure in their relationships.

There are different kinds of abuse. The next few chapters discuss some of them.

7

Verbal Abuse

Some women may look like they have their act together, but are being verbally abused. A significant other may repeatedly say things like she is too fat, skinny, or ugly. Such comments lead many women to spend all their time trying to gain weight, lose weight, putting in a new weave, taking out a new weave, or buying new clothes. In other words, constantly trying to please someone who, in reality, probably doesn't care about her anyway. Believe it or not, you may not have a secret. Somebody probably knows he's verbally abusive or suspects something is going on.

8

Physical Abuse

Here's one that we say is so awful, but all abuse is awful. The shameful part is that before someone becomes physically abused, they've probably been verbally abused. They are called out of their name and made to feel that no one else wants them. The man wants her to feel he's the best thing since apple pie, and she can't make it without him. So she constantly tells herself it's going to get better and stays. But it seldom gets better.

People who do not experience physical abuse many find it difficult to believe someone is being physically abused. That may sound ridiculous, but men who physically abuse women often become quite good at where they direct their abuse, choosing places that can be easily hidden by long sleeves—even in very hot weather. Women dealing with physical abuse may be so ashamed that she covers not only her bruises but her significant other's actions by making excuses for those injuries not as easy to hide. Like explaining a black eye by saying she ran into a door. Despite suspicions, people may not learn how severe the abuse was until the woman is hospitalized. Or killed.

One of the worst choices a woman with children can make is

to stay in an abusive relation. She may think that she is keeping the family together, but she's actually tearing her family apart. It doesn't matter how hard you strive to give your children a two-parent home; abuse will outweigh it all. Abuse is something that stays with children for a lifetime. Remember, children live what they learn.

A woman who is physically abused—or abused in any form— may wake up one day and wonder why her children have not reached their highest potential. It could be that the chain of abuse has kept them bound to the ground.

9

Controller Abuse

What do you think about someone who wants to know another's every move? It sounds like someone who wants to control a significant other's life. He talks negatively about her family members and may not even want her to spend time with them. He has studied her enough to convince her that when things are not going well with their relationship, it is because people hate them. And possibly her most of all. Yeah right. Only the person being manipulated believes that.

A controlling person of any kind is probably trying to take control of the other person's thinking. We all need to be aware of anyone with whom we can't be ourselves or we must constantly report to. If she has to report her whereabouts like a child, or someone has to know her every move, or she's been tracked, could possibly be in a relationship with someone attempting to control her.

10

Sexual Abuse

How many women do you know have been sexually abused? Probably more than you know. Women hide these things because they don't want to be looked at in a negative light. How many women in years past were told not to tell about abuse because their pasts would be revealed, and people may think she was asking for it? This type of abuse has taken place in homes, workplaces, schools, churches, playgrounds, and vacations—anywhere people gather or live. Many women have been abused on dates but are ashamed to tell about it for fear of not being believed or having someone say that they were asking for what happened to them. The latest women's movement has made it possible for women to speak out about being abused.

The sad part about it is that other women will say things like, "Why didn't she say something before now? Why did she keep it for all of these years?" Ask yourself the same question about some secret you may be carrying. As with any kind of abuse, women tend to shy away because of criticism from others.

11

Authority Abuse

Take a look around you at some workplaces and see the abuse going on. Some women shrug it off to keep their jobs. More than half the time women don't say anything for fear of losing their jobs or of someone saying they were asking for it. There are those in charge who mistreat those under them to the highest. It's kind of bad to say, but you almost have to be rude on the job to get along with some of the people who have a little authority. Please don't show a little weakness, or in some cases, you will get totally walked over.

This type of behavior can take place in the workplace regardless of what type of work it is or who's in charge. There are some so-called bosses who have no compassion when employees get sick, need to go to the doctor, or when their children or spouses get sick. Or these bosses are just plain rude.

Isn't it amazing that what goes around does come back around? Many so-called supervisors who mistreated others were fired or had to leave a job in shame. Many bosses even pretended that they were taking retirement when, in reality, they were dismissed.

Pretending Not to Know He's in Another Relationship

This is another good one. Have you met a new love? What questions are you asking? Or are you so desperate that you don't want to know? When you meet someone, and you like the person and he likes you, what's one of the first things you want to know? Not the e-mail address, not the person's favorite food, not his mother's name. Most likely you want to know how old the person's age, where they live, and their relationship status.

If a person will not tell you where he or she lives, you might want to find out why immediately. Remember that separated is not divorced. In reality, you may be running around with someone's husband and may not know it. Don't allow such a person to waste your time. An unfaithful person will tell all kinds of untruths, and before you know it, you have become entangled in a web of lies.

I once heard a guy say, "Women are so dumb." I thought it was insulting until he told me how he meant it. He was simply saying that some women don't want to know the truth or pretend not to know the truth. He later explained that he felt women don't ask enough questions. In many cases, they just go along to get along, not actually wanting to know the truth. That was just his opinion which he has a right to have.

Sometimes a friend who didn't listen and was burned can help you see a player before you even realize you are being played. Even better than that, listen to your inner self. Usually a person can sense when something is not as it should be.

13

Pretending to Be Happily Divorced

Now listen, if you are happily divorced, you don't have to tell everybody. Just be happily divorced. The funny thing is that if you left someone, why not go on with your life. If they left you, just go on with your life. There's no need to try and prove anything. You don't have to prove right. Right will prove itself. Wrong is the one that's always needing to be manipulated. Go on with life; do not be constantly talking about what someone did year after year. Instead learn to live a good and productive life. Don't worry about someone who may have wronged you in a relationship because there's one thing that can be absolutely true: Life has a way of allowing you to revisit your errors.

If you need to brag about being divorced but are constantly calling an ex, looking for any excuse to see him, constantly talking about how bad he was to anybody who will listen, or telling a new relationship how terrible the ex was, then you probably haven't gotten past those hurts as much as you pretend.

Another thing. If you are constantly calling an ex because of a child or children, you probably haven't moved on. No responsible person has to be called constantly to be told about his or her children. And when the child or children are grown, it's not an ex's responsibility to keep someone up on the grandchildren or what's going on in the children's lives, sending pictures and constantly being in contact. You don't have to keep anyone up on anything or anybody he or she has an interest in. No responsible person needs to be reminded of a child's birthday.

Take your time, and get yourself together before seeking a new relationship. Don't be pressured by those around you who are trying to rush you into another unsuccessful relationship. Do things at your pace. Don't run from one bad relationship to another. Taking your time is a major factor in having a successful relationship.

When you have actually moved on, it shows. Actions speak the loudest.

14

Pretending to Be So Self-Sufficient

Pretending to be self-sufficient is good in itself, but everybody needs someone. There is no such thing as being able to do everything yourself. Look around. Every man, woman, boy, or girl needs some type of help at one time or another. No one can do everything for themselves all the time. I once heard someone say they could pay for all of their mistakes. That's almost like saying, "I've got everything covered in life." Admit that you are not a perfect being. Anyone who totally isolates himself or herself will surely live a lonely life. The pretender is always saying he or she doesn't need anyone but are constantly secretly looking, wishing and hoping, singing and praying that God will send someone.

15

Pretending to Be a Good Friend

You already know there are some people who don't really care for you and some people you don't care for. Find people who celebrate being in your presence. There is nothing better than having a good friend to talk to. You don't want a friend who, as soon as you get off the phone with them, is calling someone else to talk about you. And you don't want a bad-weather friend. That's one who will only call when things are going sour with him or her or having a problem. You want a friend who may not necessarily agree with you on all issues, but someone you can confide in and won't tell your business all over town. And with whom you like to share things.

16

Pretending to Be So Good, Now

How many people do you know who pretend to be so good now. I say "now" because most people want to be considered good. I've often heard a pastor advising, "Don't get brand new." Simply put, meaning, now that you don't drink, smoke, steal, or whatever you used to do, you don't have to worry about that broken-down car, or you can pay your rent before the late fees. So now you want to pretend that you, on your own, have the perfect plan for life and have been blessed because of your greatness and knowledge.

Don't think you are successful all by yourself. You may never know who saw you in your craziness and said a prayer for you, or often lifted you up for God to help you. If you think back, people were probably saying the same thing about you at one time that you say about others who are struggling. Don't be so hard on people. Remember, you may have been that person at some point in your life. Why not pray more for others rather than criticize them.

Perhaps you are not that former person because someone prayed for you or helped you along life's journey. The person you are criticizing may be the person who was, at one time, looking at your craziness.

17

Pretending to Be So Healthy

I used to see a young television personality bragging about how healthy she was. She constantly talked about all the sanitizer she used and how she wiped down the airplane seat when she flew. She went on and on. Great! In a way, it's good, but why the bragging?

Most people are healthy at one point in their lives. When you are young, you can flaunt your cuteness and your health. Then life can say, "Surprise," on your health. But, you will always have the group that knows all the answer about health until something comes upon them. Wouldn't it be better to just take the best possible care of yourself and not brag about how healthy you are?

In the event you are healthy, you need to thank God, not brag.

There are people who live to be eighty or ninety years old and didn't have any exercise routine and still don't have one. Perhaps they didn't wipe all of the seats, had a drink or two when they liked, and even smoked at times. It's great to do all of the so-called good things, but in reality, just do you. Life really is short. When a person is having a health challenge, it is not necessary to have people talking about how bad he or she looks. The person has a mirror. If you don't have anything good to say, just be quiet. It's only God's grace that you are not walking in the same shoes.

18

Pretending to Love Your Coworkers

Now this is a sticky topic. We all know there are coworkers who work your last nerve. You've always got a group or one or two who are always telling others they don't need that job. Even better, they pretend not to like the boss but are doing everything in their power to get the boss' favor. Some even go so far as to talk on both sides of the fence, meaning they tell the boss on someone and then tell that person on the boss.

Probably one of the best ways to get along on the job without having to do so much pretending is just to follow your job description to the best of your ability.

A person can meet great people and develop lasting friendships on the job because that's where we spend so much of our time. But you don't have to go to the job and tell all your personal business. And then you get angry when you hear it again, especially since you were the one who told it in the beginning.

You don't have to pretend to love your coworkers. Just respect them.

19

Pretending to Love a Mate's Child from Another Relationship

Are you in a relationship in which your mate had a child with someone else. First I want to say, isn't it amazing how half the time you can't see eye to eye with your biological child or children and then pretend with your mate that you are so in love with his or her child/children from a previous relationship? Many women don't dislike the child, but they don't want to deal with the former significant other who was in her mate's life. Why? Because sometimes there are so many unresolved issues and drama.

You don't have to pretend to be better than the child's parent because one thing is a fact: You can't replace a parent, regardless of what you try. When people are considering getting into what they call a "blended family," just know your place. You don't have to pretend because if you love the child/children, your actions will tell all. Just know your place, and don't try to replace a parent.

20

Pretending to Have Another Personality

You don't have to laugh at everybody's joke. Everything is not funny. Have you ever considered that good self-esteem might just be feeling good about yourself, not trying to please everyone and go to everything. You may wake up one day and wonder what happened to you. Perhaps you spent you entire life trying to please others. Just be who you are, and most important, learn to take care of yourself. Life truly is short, so just be who you were born to be.

21

Dealing with Outright Pretenders

Don't be impressed by big houses, big cars, or even those wearing fine clothes because you never know who's living in pretense. Look around you and ask, "Am I being fooled by someone who is in debt up to his or her neck or have pulled everything out of their savings just to stay afloat and impress?" People are usually not going to tell you what they are doing. So just be careful that you are not admiring a pretender who is struggling as much as you are.

In conclusion, don't be so impressed by material things, vacations, and those pretending to live so high and mighty. Or those pretending to have all of life's answers and to have the perfect life. You may look up one day and be deeply disappointed that you were following a true pretender, who is having the same struggles as you are.

Printed in the United States
by Baker & Taylor Publisher Services